Japanese Children's Day and the Obon Festival

Dianne M. MacMillan

Reading Consultant:

Michael P. French, Ph.D.
Bowling Green State University

—*Best Holiday Books*—

Enslow Publishers, Inc.

40 Industrial Road   PO Box 38
Box 398   Aldershot
Berkeley Heights, NJ 07922   Hants GU12 6BP
USA   UK
http://www.enslow.com

Acknowledgments

The author wishes to thank Rev. Marvin Harada, Orange County Buddhist Church for his generous help.

Library of Congress Cataloging-in-Publication Data

MacMillan, Dianne., 1943-
    Japanese Children's Day and the Obon Festival / Dianne M. MacMillan.
        p. cm. — (Best holiday books)
    Includes index.
    Summary: Describes the history, customs, significance, and traditions of Japanese Children's Day and the Obon Festival, and the ways they are celebrated today in Japan and the United States.
    ISBN 0-89490-818-9
    1. Japan—Social life and customs—Juvenile literature. 2. Japan—Religious life and customs—Juvenile literature. 3. Kodomo no hi—Juvenile literature. 4. Ullambana— Juvenile literature. 5. Japanese Americans—Social life and customs— Juvenile literature. [1. Children's Day (Japan) 2. Ullambana. 3. Japan—Social life and customs. 4. Japanese Americans—Social Life and customs.]
    I. Title. II. Series
    DS821.M19 1997
    952—dc21

                        96-39170
                           CIP
                           AC

Illustration Credits: Dianne M. MacMillan, pp. 13, 15, 18, 19, 23, 24, 25, 26, 28, 31, 41, 43; James R. MacMillan, pp. 4, 6, 7, 16, 21, 22, 27, 33, 35, 36, 38, 42; Motoko Roney, p. 8.

Cover Illustration: James R. MacMillan

Contents

Fish streamers fly in the breeze on Children's Day.

Flying Fish

Huge fish-shaped streamers fly from flag poles. The streamers flap and wave in the breeze. As the wind blows, the fish swell with air. They look as if they are alive. Below the tall flag poles, hundreds of Japanese Americans have come together. Children are everywhere, laughing and playing. It is a special day for them. There are games and crafts. Actors perform special plays. Japanese drums beat out rhythms. Everyone is celebrating Japanese Children's Day. Every Spring on May 5, this holiday honors boys and girls.

In July another Japanese celebration takes

Young and old dance together and celebrate Obon.

place. This is the Obon (oh-bone) Festival. During Obon, Japanese remember their ancestors. They honor the memories of loved ones who have died. There is also a joyous festival. Food, games, and wonderful folk dances mark the day. Young and old dance together and celebrate Obon. Let's find out more about these two Japanese holidays.

Japanese performers celebrate by beating their drums.

These girls are celebrating Hina Matsuri in the traditional way.

Special Days for Children

Parents and grandparents of Japanese Americans were born in the country of Japan. Japan is a nation of islands in the Pacific Ocean. To the west are the countries of South Korea, North Korea and China. To the north is Russia.

The Japanese holiday Children's Day is celebrated on May 5. It grew out of two separate holidays, Girls' Day and Boys' Day. For over one hundred years these two holidays were celebrated. Today Children's Day combines parts of both of them.

In Japan, Girls' Day is called Hina Matsuri (HEE-nah MAHT-soo-ree). Hina means special dolls. Matsuri means festival. On March 3, a tea party is given for girls and their special set of dolls. The set might have as many as fifteen dolls or more. Sometimes the dolls are very old. Many times the dolls are passed down from mother to daughter. When the daughter grows up she gives the dolls to her daughters. The dolls are stored away for safekeeping.

A week or two before the holiday, mother and daughter unpack the dolls. Mother places the dolls on shelves built like steps. A red cloth covers the steps. Two dolls are put on the top shelf. They represent the emperor and empress, the rulers of Japan. On each side of the royal couple are two small lanterns.

Other dolls are placed below the emperor and empress. There are ladies-in-waiting, court ministers, and musicians. The dolls wear beautiful clothes made of silk. Doll furniture is placed on the lowest shelf. The sides of the steps are decorated with peach blossoms, a symbol of beauty.

On the morning of the holiday, girls dress in

traditional Japanese clothes called kimonos (kee-mow-nos). A kimono is a loose robe with wide sleeves. A large sash, called an obi, is tied around the waist. When everything is ready, the tea party begins. Girls entertain friends and neighbors. The guests want to see the dolls. Tea is poured for the visitors. There is also cake with pink and green icing. As it grows dark, the lanterns on the top shelf are lit. Because this is a special night, girls are allowed to stay up later.

Many people believe the idea for Girls' Day started thousands of years ago. At that time Japanese people believed evil spirits covered them during the long winter. When Spring came, people held a ceremony. The purpose was to clean away the evil spirits. First they made small paper dolls. Then they rubbed the dolls over their bodies. They believed this action made the evil spirits leave. The spirits moved from their bodies to the paper dolls. The dolls were then thrown into the river. Peach trees bloomed at the same time of year. Sometimes this day was called Peach Blossom Festival.

As time went on people used clay dolls instead of paper. Craftsmen made such pretty dolls, no one wanted to throw them away. About two hundred years ago craftsmen began to model the dolls after ancient Japanese royalty. They created an emperor, an empress, court attendants, servants, dogs, furniture, and orange trees for the royal garden.

These small dolls have become family treasures. Wealthy parents buy a complete set of fifteen dolls when their daughters are born. Many people save to buy a few dolls. Each year for several days people enjoy looking at the dolls.

Two months after Girls' Day, families set aside a special day for boys. Boys' Day, on May 5, is called tango-no-sekku (tahn-go-no-seck-koo). A month before Boys' Day, fathers put up a bamboo pole in the family garden. At the top of the pole they attach a pinwheel. Below the pinwheel they attach a pulley to hoist up streamers. A streamer is flown for each boy in the family. The streamers are windsocks. They look like carp, a kind of fish. The carp have open

A streamer is flown for each boy in the family.

mouths. When the wind blows, the carp streamers fill with air. As they flap in the breeze, they look alive. The carp streamers come in many different sizes and colors. The largest carp stands for the oldest boy in the family. It is placed right under the pinwheel. Just as dolls are handed down from mother to daughter, carp streamers are handed down from father to son.

Carp are very strong fish. Before they lay their eggs, they swim upstream against strong rushing water. Parents hope their sons will grow up to have qualities of the carp—strength, courage, and purpose.

Inside the house the family sets out small toy men. These toy men are dressed as ancient Japanese warriors called samurai (sah-moo-rye). The samurai warriors were brave and strong. Alongside the small warriors are tiny helmets, suits of armor, swords, and spears. All of these are used to instill courage and strength. During the day, boys visit one another's homes to see other displays.

Boys are also given special treats on their day.

Samurai weapons and armor are displayed at a museum.

Often sweet rice cakes wrapped in oak leaves are eaten. They also have small round dumplings made of sticky rice. The rice is wrapped in bamboo leaves.

Some families still carry on the old tradition of two separate holidays for girls and boys. But in recent years they have been combined into one holiday, celebrated on May 5. This is called Children's Day. It features parts of both holidays. However, if a family has a set of dolls, the dolls are displayed only on March 3.

These girls are playing traditional drums.

Children's Day

In the United States carp streamers are flown for both boys and girls. The day is filled with fun things to do and special treats. Often children dress in kimonos. In cities where many Japanese Americans live, community centers have special programs for the children. Actors perform Japanese children's stories.

"Peach Boy" is a favorite story. It tells about an old woodcutter and his wife. One day they found a giant peach. Inside the peach was a baby boy. The woodcutter and his wife kept the boy. They named him Momotaro (Mow-mow-tah-row), which means peach boy in Japanese. The boy

This storyteller is telling the story of Peach Boy.

grew up and traveled to an island. Wicked ogres lived on the island. With the help of a spotted dog, a monkey, and a pheasant, he defeated the wicked ogres. The ogres gave Momotaro all their treasure. He took the treasure back to the woodcutter and his wife. They all lived happily ever after.

These children are singing Japanese songs in honor of Children's Day.

At the Japanese-American Cultural and Community Center in Los Angeles, California, thousands of Japanese-American families come together. They want to share their Japanese heritage on Children's Day. Parents want their children to learn about Japanese traditions.

Two large flag poles fly carp streamers. The streamers let everyone know it is Children's Day. Smaller streamers decorate stores and booths. Some booths have Japanese paintings and crafts. Other booths sell beautiful decorated fans and pottery.

Japanese performers entertain visitors. Children and their parents watch karate (kah-rah-tay), judo (joo-doe), and kendo (ken-doe). These are Japanese martial arts. Martial arts began as a way for samurai warriors to train during times of peace. Kendo is Japanese fencing. Swords were important weapons of the samurai warriors. A warrior held the sword with both hands. Today instead of swords, the fencers use bamboo sticks. They wear body armor, face masks, and special gloves. Children love taking kendo classes. They

These boys and girls are demonstrating kendo movements once used by samurai warriors.

like to pretend they are samurai warriors. It takes many hours of practice to learn kendo.

There are also taiko (tie-coe) drummers. Rows of traditional taiko drums are set up. Using sticks, drummers beat out different rhythms. After the drummers play, dancers perform graceful traditional dances.

Delicious Japanese food is for sale. There are

Booths sell Japanese crafts, paintings, and pottery.

thick noodles called udon (ooh-done) and rice. There are also many kinds of pickles and radishes. Sushi (soo-shee) is a favorite food. It is made from tiny rice patties seasoned with vinegar. A piece of raw fish is placed on top. Often the rice is rolled around a cucumber, pickle, or radish.

Craft tables are set up for children. Some

children make carp streamers. These are attached to sticks. Adults show children how to make kites. Others explain Japanese brush painting. This kind of painting creates a picture using very few brushstrokes. Each stroke is an important part of the painting.

Some children learn how to do origami (oh-ree-gah-mee). Origami is the art of folding a piece of paper into a beautiful shape. It began in

Children are making carp streamers.

Japanese gardens are considered works of art.

Japan three hundred years ago. Artists use brightly colored squares of paper. The children make birds, animals, fish, and flowers. Origami shapes are made without scissors or glue.

There are other places to visit on Children's Day. Museums and libraries have puppet shows and storytellers. Some families visit Japanese gardens. Japanese gardens are considered works

Some Japanese gardens have moon bridges. The reflection in the water looks like a full moon.

of art. The gardens contain rocks, pebbles, sand, trees, ponds, and running water. The gardens are a miniature world. Rocks represent mountains. A pond stands for the ocean. Trees symbolize a forest.

The gardens are beautiful and peaceful. Some have graceful curving bridges over small ponds. The bridges are called moon bridges. Their reflection in the water looks like a round circle or a full moon. Pathways wind around plants and small stone statues.

Often there are tiny bonsai (bone-sigh) trees. Bonsai is the Japanese art of growing tiny trees. The most common bonsai is a pine tree. The tiny trees are grown from normal seeds in pots. As the tree starts to grow, it is repotted regularly. Each

Bonsai trees live as long as one hundred years. They may be as small as two inches in height.

time the plant is repotted, the roots are trimmed. This slows the tree's growth. Fast-growing branches are also cut. The smallest bonsai trees are two inches or less in height. Others range from two inches to twenty-four inches. Bonsai trees live for a very long time. Some can last as long as one hundred years.

Children's Day is a wonderful day for boys and girls. They learn about their culture and heritage. They enjoy singing and games. It is a special time for all Japanese Americans.

This day is filled with special treats and fun things to do. Here Japanese children perform fencing using bamboo sticks, instead of swords.

This is a statue of Buddha, the enlightened one. Many Japanese Americans follow the teachings of Buddha.

Obon

Each summer in July, the Japanese celebrate Obon. Obon is a Buddhist festival. It started fourteen hundred years ago. At that time the Buddhist religion was brought to Japan from Korea. Buddhism (Boo-dism) is based on the teachings of a young prince. His name was Sakyamuni (SAHK-yah-moo-nee). He became known as Buddha (Boo-dah). Many Japanese Americans follow the teachings of Buddha and the Buddhist religion. They have small altars in their home with a statue of Buddha. They also worship at Buddhist churches or temples.

During Obon, Japanese Buddhists believe that

the spirits of dead relatives return to earth for a visit. For this reason, Obon is also called the Festival of the Dead.

In Japan, Obon is a national holiday. It begins July 13 and lasts for three days. Businesses are closed. People travel home to be with their families. Before the holiday, families clean their homes from top to bottom. They buy evergreen branches, flowers, incense, fruits, and vegetables.

When the festival begins, the family lights sticks of incense. The incense burns slowly and gives off sweet-smelling smoke. Then the family places fruit and vegetables before a small family altar. This food is an offering to the spirits of the ancestors. Then the family goes to the cemetery. On the graves they place rice cakes and other offerings to welcome spirits. When it becomes dark they light lanterns and invite their ancestors to join them. For the next two days people believe the spirits are with them.

On the last night of Obon the family says goodbye to the spirits. People who live near

Obon is a national holiday in Japan and lasts for three days.

water set a candle in a small toy boat made of
straw or wood. Then the boat is set adrift.
Afterward the people dance traditional folk
dances.

The Legend of Mogallana

The celebration of Obon is based on a legend. Buddha had ten great disciples or followers. One of them was called Mogallana (MOE-gah-lah-na). Mogallana had special powers. While in deep thought he was able to see things beyond the earth.

After his mother died he wanted to see how she was doing. With his powers he saw her in the world of Hungry Ghosts. She did not look the same. She was very thin and hungry. Mogallana could see she was starving. It upset him to see his mother suffering. He offered her a bowl of rice. His mother took the rice. When she brought the

food to her mouth, the rice turned into flames.
Now Mogallana understood why his mother was
unable to eat.

Mogallana rushed to Buddha. Buddha told
him to offer food to his fellow monks on the
fifteenth day of the seventh month. This was an
act of giving. In return Mogallana was to ask the

Hundreds of people join in the Bon Odori dancing.

monks to perform a memorial service for his mother. In this way, his mother would be saved.

Mogallana did as Buddha suggested. As a result his mother rose from the world of Hungry Ghosts. Mogallana and everybody who saw this became so happy they danced for joy.

Japanese Buddhists in the United States look forward to Obon. Instead of a three-day celebration, Obon is celebrated over several weekends. The Sunday closest to July 15 is set aside to honor family members who have died. A special memorial service is held in the Buddhist temple. The minister talks about the meaning of Obon. Japanese Americans pay their respects to elders and ancestors. They remember the love, care, and kindness of their parents and grandparents. They also think about the hardships and sacrifices that their ancestors made for them. Then the minister reminds everyone about the teachings of Buddha. Those teachings help believers to rise above their sadness and problems.

On the next weekend a festival is held.

Everyone comes to celebrate with food and dancing. The dances that are part of Obon are called Bon Odori (Bone Oh-doo-re). Odori is the Japanese word for dance. Bon Odori are folk dances that are very old. The disciple Mogallana danced for joy when his mother was saved. Japanese believe his dance was the original Bon Odori. In the United States, Bon Odori have

Lanterns are a Buddhist symbol of kindness to all living things. Paper lanterns decorate the area for Bon Odori.

become an important part of the Obon celebration. Weeks before Obon, odori teachers teach some of the dances. Many of the dances are the same. But every year new ones are added.

Years ago the taiko drum was used to summon people to the temple.

Before the festival begins, a high platform or tower is built in a large open area. It represents the watch towers used long ago in Japanese villages. A taiko drum is placed on the tower.

Years ago the taiko drum summoned people to the temple. People also chanted sacred words in time with the beat of the drums. During the Bon Odori, dancers move in a circle around the tower to the beat of the drum. Paper lanterns decorate the tower and the surrounding area. The lanterns are a Buddhist symbol of kindness to all living things.

Obon festivals are social events. Church members come together to enjoy one another's company. They share their Japanese culture. Other Americans and non-Buddhists join in the celebration. In cities where many Japanese Americans live, there is more than one festival. Bon Odori dances are held at different temples each weekend from July 15 until August 15. Japanese newspapers print the schedules. Families may go to several Obon celebrations.

In the afternoon there are performances by taiko drummers.

Bon Odori

In the afternoon there are carnival games and performances by taiko drummers. Some Japanese-American children learn to play taiko drums. They practice many hours each week. Their family and friends look forward to their performances.

Before the dances begin, most everyone eats. There is a variety of delicious Japanese food. Sukiyaki (soo-kee-yah-kee) is made from strips of beef, vegetables, bean curd, and noodles. All of it is cooked quickly. A sauce, made from soybeans and sugar, is added. Soybeans are an important part of Japanese food. They are made into a paste or into a cake. The curd, which looks like cheese, is called tofu. It is eaten hot or cold. Sashimi (sah-shee-mee) is raw fish cut into bite-size chunks. The chunks are dipped in a sauce and eaten. Rice is served with the other foods. Wooden chopsticks come with the food. Non-Japanese visitors have fun trying to eat with chopsticks.

Many women and men dress in traditional kimonos. Others wear a yukata (yoo-kah-tah), a thin cotton garment that is shorter than a kimono. Because Obon takes place in the summer, the yukata is more comfortable. Some people wear geta (geh-tah) instead of shoes. Geta are clogs with wooden blocks on the bottom. The clogs were worn long ago in Japan because the roads were often very muddy.

Short, loose jackets called happi (hahp-pee) coats are also worn. They are made in bright colors. Some have designs on them. Temple and church groups make happi coats for their people to wear when taking part in festivals. Each

These children are dressed in traditional kimonos.

temple chooses different colors for their happi coats. The coats are tied around the waist.

As the sun goes down, it is time for Bon Odori to begin. Hundreds of people gather into large circles. The drums and music begin. Dancers move around the circle. With the dancers' colorful kimonos and happi coats, the circle looks like a giant pinwheel.

Dancers use round fans made of bamboo.

Sometimes as many as five hundred people dance together. Bon Odori is not just for Buddhists. Anyone can join in. Bon Odori brings people together from different backgrounds and religions.

The dances tell the stories of Japanese villagers. Some are about a fisherman, a coal miner, and a farmer harvesting rice. The dances are easy to learn. With hand movements and simple steps the dancers move around the circle. Each dance has four or five simple movements set to music. The steps are repeated over and over again. One dance uses round fans made of bamboo. In another dance, the dancers hold two pairs of bamboo sections called kachi-kachi

This family dances every year at the Obon festival.

(kah-chee kah-chee). The click clack of the kachi-kachi, as they are hit together, join the beat of the taiko drums.

When the last dance is over, the "pinwheel" circles come to a stop. Some families will dance again next weekend at another temple. Others will wait for next year. But the happy memories of Obon will stay with them.

Japanese Americans enjoy their festivals. Children's Day and Obon bring families together. The food, music, and joyous dancing make everyone proud of his or her heritage. They look forward to next year's celebrations.

Glossary

ancestors—People from whom one is descended.

bonsai—The art of growing miniature trees.

culture—Customs, beliefs, and arts of a distinct group of people.

disciple—A person who follows and believes in a leader and his teachings.

geta—Wooden clogs worn on the feet.

happi coat—Short, loose jackets worn by people who belong to Buddhist church groups.

heritage—Customs, achievements, and history passed on from earlier generations; Tradition.

kendo—Japanese-style fencing using bamboo sticks.

kimono—A loose-fitting wide-sleeved robe worn by Japanese women and men. It is tied at the waist with a sash.

legend—A story told over and over. Many people believe in legends even though they are not always true.

martial arts—Self-defense methods from Asia.

obi—A large sash tied around the waist.

ogre—A man-eating giant in fairy tales and folklore.

origami—The art of folding squares of paper into shapes.

samurai—Ancient Japanese warriors.

sashimi—Raw fish cut into bite-sized chunks.

sukiyaki—Strips of beef, vegetables, bean curd, and noodles cooked quickly.

sushi—Tiny rice patties with a piece of raw fish on top.

yukata—A light cotton garment that resembles a robe. It is shorter than the traditional kimono and worn in the summer time.

Index

B

Bon Odori, *33*, 35, 36, 37, 42

bonsai, 26, 27

Boys' Day, 9, 12–16

Buddha, *28*, 29, 32, 33, 34

Buddhism, 29, 32-34, 42

C

Children's Day, 5, 7, 9, 16, 27, 44

G

geta shoes, 40

Girls' Day, 9–12

H

happi coats, 40, 41

Hina Matsuri, 8, 9-12

J

Japan, 9, 10

judo, 20